Children's Party Cake Book

By Cathy Mackinlay.

MEREHURST PRESS
LONDON

The Party Cake is the feature of the Birthday table setting. Children of all ages, need to feel special on this day by having their name emblazoned on an edible confection, and to see the candles lit and relit to the delight and puff of their friends.

Some of my favourite recipes are included in this book, but do use your own favourites if it makes life easier. Uncomplicated no-fuss icing recipes are essential. If in doubt make more than the recipe states, as Buttercream Icing will keep several weeks in the freezer and Royal Icing will keep approximately 2 weeks in a sealed container.

Many Cake Decorating books are on the market now, and this is wonderful for ideas and inspiration. Most children have favourite toys and characters, and these can be copied by combining sectioned cakes and icings and colours.

While teaching cake decorating to many pupils I always loved the pleasure they achieved from modelling the fondant icing like plasticine or playdough or clay. They marvelled that it was so easy once they got over the initial hurdle of "Oh, I could never do that!"

My ideas of combining the Buttercream with the Fondant Icing achieve remarkable effects and almost any shape imaginable.

The Cake Decorating programmes I did on television made me realise that there are many people interested in this subject in so many distant places. These people should not feel too remote or isolated as most shops will freight their products to your door. National magazines contain advertisements from most Cake Decorating shops.

The joy on the faces of the children receiving their cakes, is the greatest satisfaction, and I would like this book to be a delight for children to look at and read over and over again.

I would like to thank my mother and my friends for minding my two small children while I covered the cakes and my house with icing. But remember, after all this lovely lovely icing a crunchy apple, or a toothbrush is essential for growing teeth!!

Cathy Mackinlay

Cake Recipes

Most people have their favourite cake recipes and all the cakes in this book can be modified by the use of your own recipes.

The four recipes used throughout this book, were given to me by friends and are excellent. Their usage is recommended.

COMMERCIAL CAKE MIXES

Most commercial cake mixes can be baked either in a conventional oven, or a microwave oven. The microwave definitely speeds up the birthday cake making process, but I do find that a microwave cake will tend to go stale more quickly, especially after 24 hours. However most cakes are consumed far too quickly for the staling process to occur!

CHOCOLATE CAKE

1½ cups flour
¼ cup cornflour
¾ tsp baking powder
½ cup cocoa
½ tsp soda
1½ cups sugar
125g melted butter
¾ cup milk
2 eggs
1 tsp vanilla

Sift all dry ingredients together into a large bowl and make a well in the centre. Add the melted butter, milk, eggs and vanilla essence and mix together at a medium speed for three minutes. Bake in two lined round 18cm tins for 30—35 minutes at 180degC. This cake can also be baked in a swiss roll tin for approximately 40 minutes.

SULTANA CAKE

450gms sultanas
sufficient water to cover
225gms butter
325gms sugar
3 eggs
325gms flour
1 tsp baking powder
1 tsp vanilla essence
1 tsp lemon essence
1 tsp almond essence

Wash sultanas in a pan and cover with water. Boil, then simmer for 5 minutes. Strain, then pour the hot fruit into the softened butter. Beat together the sugar and eggs until soft and creamy. Sift in the flour and baking powder. Add the essences, and combine with the fruit and butter mixture.

Bake in a lined 20cm square cake tin for 1½ hours at 180degC.

SPICY APPLE CAKE

2 medium apples, chopped
1 cup sugar
1 egg
½ cup melted butter
1½ cups flour
1 tsp baking soda
½ tsp salt
1 tsp cinnamon
½ tsp nutmeg
½ tsp allspice
1 cup sultanas

Place the chopped apples in a medium sized bowl, pour the sugar over the top, stir, and leave for 10 minutes. Add the egg and melted butter and stir well. Add the remaining ingredients and mix thoroughly. Finally add the sultanas. Pour into a lined 20cm round cake tin. Bake for 50 minutes at 180degC.

Leave the cooked cake in the tin until cold. It is firmer and easier to handle when cold.

LESLEY'S BANANA CAKE

2 bananas
3 tbsp milk
1 tsp baking soda
1 egg
1 tsp baking powder
1 heaped cup flour
112g butter
1 cup sugar

Heat the bananas to a cream and stir in the milk and soda. Cream the butter and sugar, beat in the egg, then fold in the dry ingredients and the banana mixture. Combine well. Bake for 50 mins to 1 hr at 180degC in a 20cm lined, either round or square tin.

THE ABOVE FOUR CAKES COOKED IN A CONVENTIONAL OVEN WILL STAY FRESH FOR AT LEAST THREE DAYS. REMEMBER, HOWEVER, THAT THE ADDITION OF FRESHLY WHIPPED CREAM WILL REDUCE THE LASTING QUALITY.

THE ABOVE ARE THE BASIC CAKE RECIPES USED THROUGHOUT THIS BOOK.

PREPARATION OF THE NOVELTY SHAPED CAKES

Once the cake has been baked, preparation of the novelty shape is the next task.

Recently, CAKE DECORATING shops sell, as well as hire out, specially shaped tins. For a busy mother preparing for a party, it is usually essential to save time, and these commercial shapes are a boon. As cutting into a cake tends to dry the edges very quickly, the least amount of slicing possible should be done. Therefore the use of specially shaped tins is recommended. e.g. In SECTION 6 tins are available for all numerals. Also available are the HORSE and XMAS TREE tins. After the shape has been created the icing is the next important step.

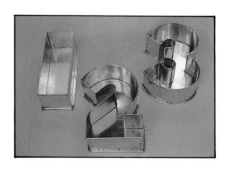

ICINGS

There are many variations of the following recipes, but simplicity is the keynote.

MARZIPAN

225g icing sugar
225g castor sugar
125g ground almonds
2 egg yolks
1 lightly beaten egg white
1 tsp lemon juice
2 tsp almond essence

Combine all ingredients and stir well. Turn out on to a board sprinkled with icing sugar and knead until it is like dough, adding more icing sugar if necessary. It should be of a good rolling consistency. If too dry add a little more lemon juice or sherry. Keep wrapped in plastic or gladwrap to prevent drying out.

Commercial almond paste or marzipan can be bought from grocers, supermarkets or cake decorating shops.

ROYAL ICING

This icing is mostly used for formal decorations and wedding cakes. It sets rock hard, must not be chilled or frozen, and will keep for 2 weeks at the most in a sealed container.

1 egg white (at room temperature)
1¼ to 1½ (approx) cups pure icing sugar
2–4 drops lemon juice or glacial acetic acid
colouring (if required)

Place the white in a bowl and using a small wooden spoon (NEVER an electric beater) add the sifted icing sugar two tablespoons at a time beating well after each addition. Add the lemon juice and beat well. If colouring is required, add very carefully drop by drop. Take extra care with the addition of powdered dyes as they are very intense and tend to develop more intensely over a period of two to three days. Therefore to avoid "spotting" colour your icings well before hand.

BUTTERCREAM ICING

250g butter
500g icing sugar
1 tbsp cream or milk

Slightly soften the butter then beat the three ingredients together until creamy. Colourings should now be added drop by drop until the desired intensity is achieved. This icing tends to darken slightly after approximately half an hour on the cake.

All the recipes in this book allow for extra Buttercream Icing and any excess can be frozen for a few weeks, or kept cool in a refrigerator for as long as you would keep butter. This icing is the favourite of children and adults alike.

FONDANT ICING

There are many good recipes available for fondant icing but for easy use there are good products on the market. Make sure the icing is soft before you purchase it. The icing should have the same feel as the well known "playdough". Commercial Fondant will keep approximately two months, if kept well wrapped in plastic, but do NOT refrigerate.

To colour the fondant always begin with one or two drops of liquid colouring and a small fist sized piece of icing, knead well, and if this becomes sticky use a small amount of cornflour to assist with the kneading process.

Powdered dyes should be added to the fondant in very small amounts e.g. the amount you can pile on the end of a toothpick. Knead well with your two forefingers, leave several hours, and you will see small "dots" of intense colour "developing". Knead again, and repeat this process over the next two days.

To attach two fondant surfaces together they can be dampened with a small amount of water.

To achieve a good Xmas red the powdered dye is essential, the liquid dye never achieves the same intensity. All Cake Decorating shops should have black and red powdered dyes.

PLAYDOUGH

This is an excellent quick recipe and keeps little hands busy while you are modelling the real fondant!

½ cup salt
1 cup flour
2 tsp cream of tartar
1 tbsp oil
1 cup water
food colouring

Combine all ingredients in a saucepan, warm slightly, and stir until a dough is formed.

This playdough keeps approximately two weeks in a plastic bag, or for as long as it is kept out of sand, mud, ashes, water, grass, and other extraneous matter children love!

EQUIPMENT

Cake Decorating shops these days are like Wonderland. Vast arrays of ribbons, flowers, silver and gold objects, plastic animals and people indulging in all types of sport. Most shopowners are themselves decorators and like myself they love to talk about the art and give you all the hints, latest ideas and help.

For greatest ease keep the icing nozzles as few as possible. The main ones used are No. 2 for writing and a star nozzle for ropes, scrolls, stars and swirls.

Boards for my cakes are anything from pinex, carefully cut with a fretsaw by my obliging husband, to the cardboard divisions in the wine cartons!

To cover the boards there is a wonderful array of coloured shiny papers available, but make sure they are not oil absorbent or the butter in your Buttercream Icing will make nasty marks across the paper. Most boards are covered with foil. Cut a piece 4cm wider than the board all round, press the edges underneath and cellotape into position.

A small thought — there are non-extinguishable candles available which although they provide a lot of fun, can be dangerous if not soaked in water after use. Also they tend to lead to an awful lot of "puff" and other droplets on the cake.

"Eyes" are difficult to copy in icings, but realistic plastic copies are availabe in Cake Decorating and Craft Shops.

Most of all, use lots and lots of sweets and make your cakes a real delight for many pairs of small eyes!

Favourite Tales

SLEEPING BEAUTY

1 20cm square cake
500gm Fondant Icing (approx.)
4 plastic pillars
boiled lollies
marshmallows
2 scorched almonds
2 chocolate fingers
food colourings
½ recipe of Royal Icing
1 recipe of Buttercream Icing
   (chocolate)

Cover the top and sides of the cake with a thin layer of Chocolate Buttercream Icing.

Roll out 2 strips of fondant icing for the visible parts of the white bed sheets and pillow. Make the pillow 3cm x 2cm. Press the sheets and pillow into position at the top of the cake. Place two chocolate fingers and two scorched almonds in position for legs and feet.

Colour the remaining Fondant Icing with pink food colouring and roll it out to fit the bed overlapping the sides gently. Press the pink blanket over the "body" and pinch the blanket edges for a wave-like effect.

Colour some Pink Fondant Icing red and curl up small pieces to form 27 roses pressed into 9 separate bunches of 3 roses each. Shape a small mouth of Red Fondant and press onto the face.

With White Royal Icing and a No. 2 icing nozzle, pipe flowers onto the blanket, pipe the blanket edging and attach the sweets to the end of the bed.

Pipe her hair and eyes with Chocolate Buttercream and a No. 2 icing nozzle.

Green Royal Icing is piped amongst the roses to make small leaves.

Arrange the candles, roses and pillars around the cake.

TREASURE CHEST
1 chocolate cake recipe
1 recipe buttercream coloured with
   ½ tsp Yellow food colouring
Black Royal Icing
firm cardboard 17cm x 7.5cm
gold or yellow paper
oddfellows
money bubblegum
blackballs
boiled lollies

Bake the chocolate cake in a sponge roll tin and when cold cut into 2 width wise. Place jam and whipped cream on the top of one half and place the other half on top to represent a chest.

Cover the chest smoothly with Yellow Buttercream Icing.

Paste gold paper onto both sides of the cardboard then pipe yellow Buttercream Icing around the edge of the chest and cardboard with a star icing nozzle and icing bag.

Arrange the sweets and prop up the chest lid as in the photograph.

Pipe the word "Treasure!" onto the side of the chest with Black Royal Icing and a No. 2 icing nozzle.

TOADSTOOL AND GNOMES

1 20cm round cake (not too high)
3 x 10cm round cakes
200gm White Fondant Icing
200gm Red Fondant Icing
1 recipe of Pink Buttercream Icing
coconut coloured green
2 plastic gnomes
1 china frog
1 china toadstool set
dried flowers
cardboard circle 20cm in diameter

This popular cake looks magical! Pile the 3 10cm cakes into a "stack" with jam and whipped cream between each layer. Place the large cake onto the circle of cardboard with a small amount of jam on the cardboard to stick to the cake.

Ice the "stack" and the large cake with Pink Buttercream Icing.

Roll out the white Fondant Icing and place it carefully around the circumference of the "stack". Trim off excess icing, this is now the stem of the Toadstool.

Roll out the Red Fondant Icing into a circle 26cm in diameter and place over the larger cake overlapping the sides. Press small balls of White Fondant Icing into the red top of the Toadstool. Place this cake onto the stem.

Pipe windows and a door onto the stem with a No. 2 icing nozzle. Arrange the coconut, flowers, gnomes, frog and toadstools in any style you wish.

Diagram A

A Visible lower part of skirt

4cm

28cm

B Visible front of skirt

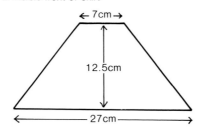

← 7cm →

12.5cm

27cm

C Apron

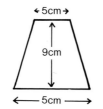

← 5cm →

9cm

5cm

Diagram B

A Skirt section

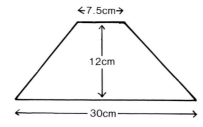

← 7.5cm →

12cm

30cm

B Cape section

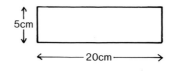

5cm

20cm

C Hood

Top

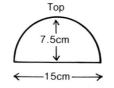

7.5cm

15cm

(Not to Scale)

RED RIDING HOOD

1 cake recipe or 1 packet cake mix
500gm White Fondant Icing
250gm Red Fondant Icing
½ recipe of White Royal Icing
½ recipe of Buttercream Icing
27cm nylon lace
5 tbs coconut, coloured green
chocolate buttons
1 doll approx. 20cm tall

Bake the cake in a well-greased, well-floured Dolly Varden tin, for longer than if the cake was baked in a square or round tin.

Invert the cake when cold, then with a knife, cut out a hole in which the cleaned doll will be placed up to her waistline. Cover the cake smoothly with Buttercream Icing.

Roll out the Fondant Icing to .5cm thick and cut 3 shapes as in diagram A.

Gently drape these 3 pieces onto the iced skirt of the doll. Cut a small piece of extra for the front belt, and model a bodice and sleeves on the front of the doll only.

Roll the Red Fondant Icing to .5cm thick and cut 3 shapes as in diagram B. Also cut thin strips for ties. Place these pieces onto the doll as in the photograph. The fondant will adhere together if dampened slightly.

Cut the lace into 3 lengths and pipe White Royal Icing onto the edge of the apron with a No. 2 icing nozzle, attaching the lace by pressing it into the icing. Pipe the dots and lines on the apron and the frilly edge of the sleeve.

Green coloured coconut and chocolate buttons represent the "grass" and "rocks" of the countryside.

HICKORY DICKORY DOCK

1 chocolate cake recipe
1 recipe Buttercream Icing
Red Royal Icing
Black Royal Icing
4 long licorice twists
hundreds and thousands
chocolate hail
pebbles

Bake the chocolate cake in a sponge roll tin, and using the width of the tin as in the diagram, make a paper circle. Trim off top edges of cake as in diagram.

Ice the whole cake smoothly with Buttercream Icing and press the pebbles into a circle using the paper pattern.

Place all the sweets onto the cake as in the photograph.

Pipe the clock's hands and numbers with Black royal Icing and a No. 2 icing nozzle. The face is piped in Red Royal Icing.

A star icing nozzle is used to pipe Buttercream Icing around the outside of the face and down the sides of the licorice.

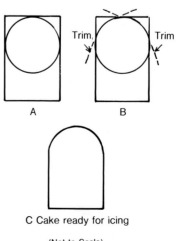

A

B

Trim   Trim

C Cake ready for icing

(Not to Scale)

HUMPTY DUMPTY

1 loaf tin cake 20cm x 7.5cm
1 recipe of Buttercream Icing
200gm White Fondant Icing
red, black, yellow colourings
chocolate hail
pebbles
coconut coloured green
blue bow
butterfly, frog, toadstools
1 licorice strap
Royal Icing

Any square or loaf cake may be used but it must have a high side to show off the brick pattern.

Reserve ½ cup of Buttercream Icing and colour the remaining with cocoa. Smooth this over the top and sides of the cake and along the pathway.

Pipe the bricks with a No. 2 icing nozzle and White Buttercream Icing.

Humpty is formed by covering a bundle of foil-wrapped sweets with Fondant Icing. Smooth into a hemispherical shape and place on the wall top. Cut the licorice to form 2 arms and 2 legs and place these under Humpty.

Colour 2tbs of Fondant Red and model hands.

Colour 2tbs of Fondant Black and model a top hat.

Colour 2tbs of Fondant Yellow and model 2 shoes.

Press these features onto the body and limbs.

Pipe a circle of White Buttercream Icing scrolls around Humpty's base and press in the blue bow.

Place all the other ingredients in position as in the photograph.

Pipe the face with Red and Black Royal Icing and a No. 2 icing nozzle.

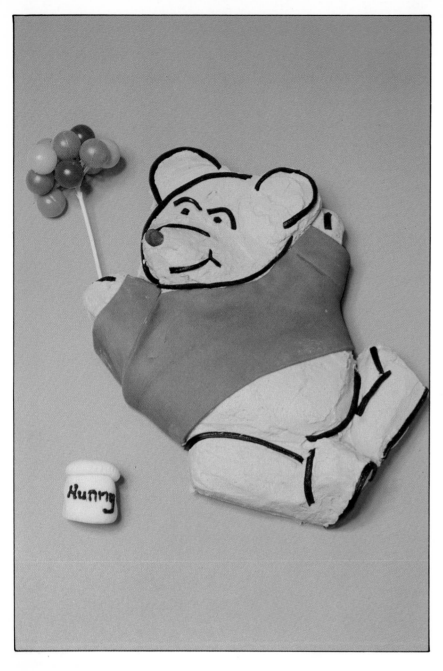

LITTLE YELLOW BEAR

1 round chocolate cake 25cm diam.
1 ½ recipe of Buttercream Icing
yellow and brown liquid food
   colourings
2 licorice straps
100gm Red Fondant Icing
4tbs Yellow Fondant Icing
Black Royal Icing
2 bees
1 bunch of plastic balloons

Cut the cake as in the diagram and use the offcuts to raise the feet, nose, ears and rounded tummy.

Mix ¾ tsp yellow food colouring and 4 drops of brown food colouring into the Buttercream Icing.

Cover the little bear completely with the Yellow Buttercream Icing.

Roll out the Red Fondant Icing to .5cm thick and cut out a jacket and 2 sleeves, then press these into position on the body.

Cut the licorice into strips and shape by pressing into the icing.

The honey pot is modelled from Yellow Fondant Icing.

With No. 2 icing nozzle, pipe the word ''Hunny'' onto the pot, also pipe the bear's eyes and nose.

25cm

(Not to Scale)

14

LITTLE MISS MUFFET

1 packet of cake mix
1 recipe of Buttercream Icing
green food colouring
assorted green sweets
Black Fondant Icing
licorice
1 doll approx. 20cm tall

Bake the cake in a Dolly Varden tin, and proceed with cutting a hole for the doll as in the Little Red Riding Hood cake.

Colour the Buttercream Icing green and smooth this with a knife all over the skirt of the doll.

With a star icing nozzle and an icing bag, pile the "bodice" of the dress and the "stars" in between the sweets as in the photograph.

Press into the skirt all the greenest sweets you can purchase!

The spider is moulded from two balls of Black Fondant Icing, the larger ball being for the body. Press eight 2.5cm long strips into the body for legs, and make eyes by pressing a toothpick into the Fondant Icing.

A "tuffet" could be made by icing a cup cake with an extra green icing.

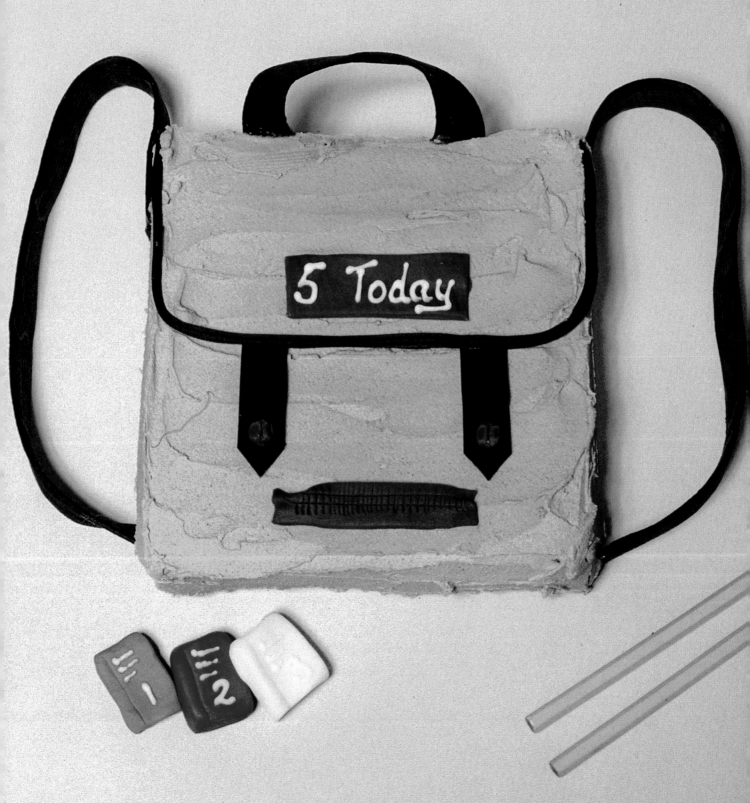

Off to School

SCHOOL BAG

1 20cm square banana cake
1 recipe of Chocolate Buttercream
    Icing
3 licorice straps
4 tbs Fondant Icing
red, yellow, green, brown food
    colourings
2 tbs White Royal Icing

Cover the square cake completely with the Chocolate Buttercream Icing.

Cut the licorice straps into a top handle, 2 side straps, 2 smaller attachment straps and a thin strip for around the opening flap. Press all these pieces into the cake while Buttercream Icing is still soft.

Divide the Fondant Icing into 4 pieces and colour each, then model into 'books' and 'label' as in the photograph.

Pipe the writing onto the books and label with White Royal Icing and using a No. 2 icing nozzle.

The unsharpened pencils are placed by the bag ready for first use.

TRAFFIC SIGNALS

1 chocolate cake recipe
1 recipe Buttercream Icing
200gm Grey Fondant Icing
coconut coloured green
traffic signs
vehicles
dried flowers
green ribbon

This chocolate cake is baked in a swiss roll tin, cooled & inverted to achieve a very flat surface. Thinly cover the top and sides of the cake with Buttercream Icing.

Prepare the Grey Fondant Icing three days before use, kneading the icing about three times a day to get a true grey. If too dark, add some extra White Fondant and knead again. Roll out to .5cm thick and cut to size for roads then press into the Buttercream Icing.

Set out the traffic signs, vehicles, coconut, dried flowers, and ribbon round the cakes.

Pipe road markings with Buttercream Icing and a No. 2 icing nozzle.

APPLE FOR THE TEACHER

1 20cm round apple cake
400gm Red Fondant Icing
1 recipe Buttercream Icing
yellow and brown food colourings
green sweets

Cover the trimmed (see diagram) cake with Buttercream Icing.

Roll out the Red Fondant Icing to .5cm thick, lay over the cake and trim the base with a small sharp knife.

Colour 2tbs of fondant brown and make a stalk for the top of the cake, and dried petals for base of apple.

The green sweets are the leaves.

The Yellow Buttercream Icing is piped onto the apple with a No. 2 icing nozzle.

Trim

Trim

(Not to Scale)

19

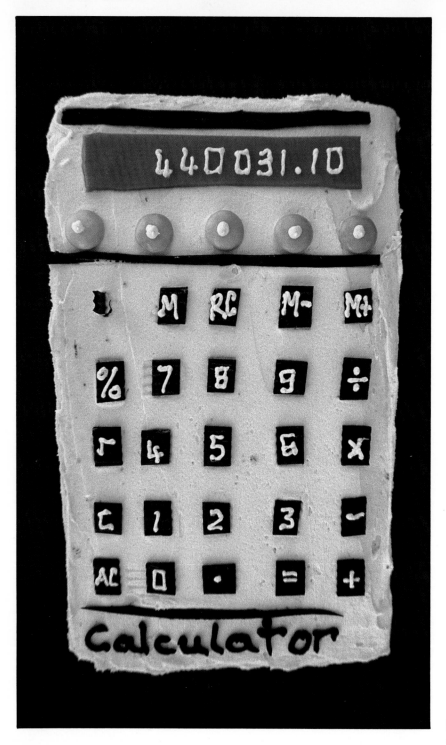

CALCULATOR

1 square or oblong cake to your size calculator
1 recipe Buttercream Icing
2 licorice straps
5 yellow pebbles
Black Royal Icing
Red Fondant Icing

Cover the cake completely with White Buttercream Icing.

Cut licorice straps into squares for the buttons and three thin strips for division lines.

Press in 5 yellow pebbles.

Roll out Red Fondant Icing and cut to size for readout.

With Buttercream Icing and a No. 2 writing nozzle pipe all the numbers and dots on the buttons.

With the Black Royal Icing and a No. 2 writing nozzle pipe the word calculator at the base of the cake.

CAKE FOR MY BEST FRIEND

1 heart-shaped tin
1 banana cake recipe
1 recipe Buttercream Icing
400gm Fondant Icing
red and pink food colourings
ribbon
plastic mouse and heart motif

Smooth Buttercream Icing over top and sides of cake.

Roll out 200gm of Pink Coloured Fondant Icing to .5cm thick, place over the cake and trim around the base with a sharp knife.

Roll out 200gm of Red Coloured Fondant to .5cm thick and using a small heart-shaped cutter, cut out 12 hearts. Also model a few rose buds around 2 stamens each.

Pipe Buttercream Icing around top and base of cake sides with a No. 2 icing nozzle, also attach hearts to cake and complete the script.

Insert mouse motif and place the ribbon wherever desired.

Sports and Hobbies

GUITAR

1 recipe of chocolate cake
guitar-shaped tin
1 recipe of Buttercream Icing and
  Cocoa
500gm Brown Fondant Icing
Black Royal Icing
black powder food colouring

Carefully grease and flour the tin and the guitar cake should come out perfectly when baked. Turn cake upside down for icing, and cover the cake completely with Chocolate Buttercream reserving 2tbs of Buttercream Icing for the 'strings' of the guitar.

Roll out the Brown Fondant icing to .5cm thick and using the tin, cut a body shape with hole in centre and another shape for the head of the guitar. Place these onto the cake.

Colour some Brown Fondant Icing darker for the pegs and the bridge base, and colour the rest of the icing black. Cut to size, lay on the cake and press in the fret markings with a knife.

Pipe Chocolate Buttercream Icing scrolls around top and base of cake with a star icing nozzle and the other markings with a No. 2 icing nozzle. Press the six pegs into the head of the guitar and lay a toothpick over the bridge base.

Carefully pipe the 'strings' with the White Buttercream Icing and a No. 2 icing nozzle.

The clef is piped with a No. 3 icing nozzle and Black Royal Icing.

The sheet music makes an interesting background.

SOCCER BALL

1 chocolate cake recipe
1 hired ball-shaped tin set
1 recipe of Buttercream Icing
200gm Black Fondant Icing
Red Royal Icing
coconut coloured green

Bake the cakes in the well-greased and floured two halves of the ball tin.

Trim to level when cool, then put together with jam and cream. Ice all over the top and sides with Buttercream Icing, then with a sharp knife press in the "stitching" lines of the ball.

Roll out the Black Fondant icing.

With a 5-sided tupperware block or similar cutter, cut out .5cm thick pieces and press these onto the Buttercream Icing.

Pipe the writing with Red Royal Icing and a No. 2 icing nozzle.

The green coloured coconut represents grass.

To keep the soccer ball anchored firmly on the board, hammer a 10cm nail up through the board from underneath and set the soccer ball carefully onto it.

SOCCER FIELD

1 recipe chocolate cake
1 recipe of Buttercream Icing
300gm Green Fondant Icing
1 plastic soccer set with goals
4 toothpicks
coloured gummed paper
White Fondant
small piece of licorice

Bake the chocolate cake in a swiss roll tin to achieve a good 'field' shape.

Ice Buttercream Icing over the top and sides of the cake.

Roll out the Green Fondant Icing to .5cm thick and cut to the size of a swiss roll tin and set onto the cake.

With a star icing nozzle pipe a scroll around the top and base of the sides of the cake, then with a No. 2 icing nozzle pipe the ball, field lines and attach players, goals and nets to the field.

Gum square pieces of coloured paper to the toothpicks to represent flags and place in position.

The extra balls are made from White Fondant Icing and tiny pieces of licorice are pressed in to make the ball more "real-looking".

NETBALL COURT

1 recipe chocolate cake
1 recipe Chocolate Buttercream
Icing
300gm Grey Fondant Icing
Royal Icing
red food colouring
licorice tube
1 beef skewer painted silver
ribbons of team colours

Ice this cake as for the soccer field except use Grey Fondant instead of Green Fondant Icing, and Brown Chocolate Buttercream instead of plain.

Label the positions with Red Royal Icing and a No. 2 icing nozzle.

The goal posts are one beef skewer painted silver, cut in half and each half topped with a thin cross section of "tube" licorice.

The team colours lie in the foreground.

CARD PLAYERS

1 23cm round sultana cake
1 beaten egg white
400gm White Fondant Icing
2 clean cards
red and black food colourings
bubblegum packets
red ribbon
red rosette
½ recipe Royal Icing

Brush the egg white lightly over the cake. Roll out the Fondant Icing to .5cm thick, measuring size carefully, and spread over the cake pressing in around the base and trimming off the excess fondant with a sharp knife. Clip carefully around top of cake with cake decorating clippers.

Colour some Fondant Icing red for hearts and diamonds, and black for the spades and clubs. Roll out these colours and cut the shapes with special cutters available from cake decorating shops.

Pipe a scroll of White Royal Icing around the base of the cake with a star icing nozzle, and adhere cards, fondant shapes, ribbon and red bow onto the cake surface.

Red Royal Icing is piped in dots around the top and base sides of the cake with a No. 2 icing nozzle. The wrapped bubble gum adds interest!

RECORD PLAYING

1 22cm round apple cake
400gm marzipan
1 recipe Chocolate Buttercream
    Icing
Royal Icing
black food colouring powder
jelly beans
2 plastic band sets

Cover the cake smoothly with the Buttercream Icing and pipe a scroll around the top and base of the sizes with a star icing nozzle. Press jelly beans into the icing on the side of the cake.

Colour the marzipan, less one tablespoon, with the black food powder three days beforehand.

Roll into a circle 22cm in diameter and .5cm thick and place this on the cake. With the serrated edge of a cake decorating ruler, swirl around to print out the 'grooves' of the record.

Make a marzipan circle and press this into the middle of the 'record' and print a message with Black Royal Icing and a No. 2 icing nozzle.

Place bands and streamers in position.

ROLLER SKATE

1 20cm square banana cake
½ recipe Buttercream Icing
300gm White Fondant Icing
60gm Red Fondant Icing
150gm Black Fondant Icing
100gm marzipan
Red Royal Icing
Non-toxic silver paint.

Cut the cake as in diagram (a) and piece together as in diagram (b) with jam or whipped cream. Smooth the Buttercream Icing over the entire cake surface.

Roll out the White Fondant Icing to .5cm thick and mould this over the boot part of the cake carefully pressing flat the top boot "opening".

Cut the Black and Red Fondant Icings to fit as in the photograph, for the under carriage, boot eyelets and patches.

Mould two wheels and a "stopper" from marzipan and press a small ball of White Fondant Icing into the centre of the wheels. Paint with silver paint.

Pipe Red Royal Icing and a No. 2 icing nozzle for "stitches" and "laces".

Diagram A (Not to Scale)

←------- 20cm -------→

(ii)

(i)

Diagram B

(i)

(ii)

←------ 20cm ------→

29

JOGGING SHOE

1 20cm diam. round chocolate cake
cream and raspberry jam
½ recipe Buttercream Icing
500gm Pale Blue Fondant Icing
100gm marzipan
Royal Icing for piping
cake decorating ruler for dots

Cut the cake as in the diagram and build up the top of the shoe and extra onto the "toe" section with (i) and (ii) cake portions. Join altogether with cream & raspberry jam.

Cover the entire cake smoothly with Buttercream Icing.

Roll out the Blue Fondant Icing to .5cm thick and lay over the cake pressing in at the bottom edges. Cut away excess icing.

Roll the icing out again and shape the top section with a knife, dampen the shoe slightly and lift the icing onto the cake. Make eyelet depressions with a beef skewer tip. Model a small tongue and press onto cake.

Make laces with long modelled strips of fondant icing. Model marzipan for decoration on shoe sides. Pipe writing onto the "tongue" with a No. 2 icing nozzle and White Royal Icing or Buttercream Icing.

Using a sharp knife press in all the shoe's decorations, stitching etc.

The cake decorating ruler has a serrated edge and easily presses into the icing to create the dotted effect.

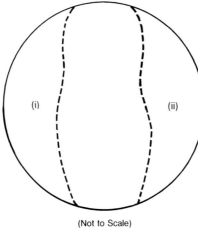

(i)   (ii)

(Not to Scale)

WIND SOCK KITE

1 sponge roll cake
400gm Fondant Icing
1 recipe of Buttercream Icing
yellow, green & red food colourings
coloured ribbons — 1 metre of each
licorice staples

Cut each ribbon into three lengths.

Cover the cake completely with Buttercream Icing, and press the ribbons into the end of the cake.

Leave ¼ of the Fondant Icing White, colour the other three parts the yellow, green and red of the ribbons and roll each out proportionately to the size of the sponge roll cake. Lay these coloured pieces together, dampen the cut edges, and join the four strips together rolling them with the rolling pin to seal the seams. Lift this whole piece onto the cake, press in the sides and trim away the excess Fondant Icing with a sharp knife.

The licorice staples add related colour and interest.

RACING CAR

1 chocolate cake recipe baked in a
   swiss roll tin
500gm White Fondant Icing
1 recipe of Buttercream Icing
1 pkt chocolate mint biscuits
8 red pebbles
licorice pieces
Royal Icing
2 x 15cm pieces of wire
silver non-toxic paint

Cut the cake as in the diagram (A) and place sections (ii) and (iii) on top of section (i) as in diagrams (B) or (C).

Cover the cake smoothly all over with Buttercream Icing.

Roll out the Fondant Icing to .5cm thick and place this carefully over the cake smoothing into the corners and edges with fingertips. Cut away excess icing with a small sharp knife.

With the White Royal Icing and a No. 2 icing nozzle and bag, pipe all the lines and dots as in the photograph. Attach the licorice, biscuits and pebbles with a spot of Royal Icing.

Paint the silver onto the cake with a toothpick when the Royal Icing is firm approximately 2 hours.

Press in the wire "aerials".

Diagram A

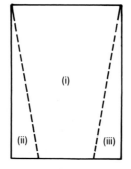

Diagram C Top view

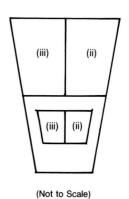

Diagram B Side view

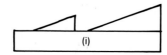

(Not to Scale)

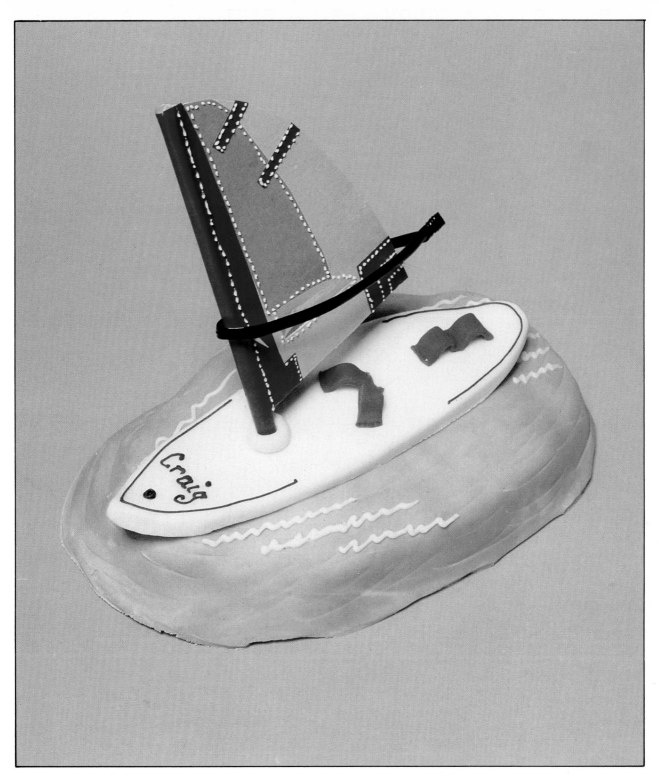

WIND SURFER

1 pkt cake mix
500gm Fondant Icing
1 recipe Buttercream Icing
red, blue and black food colourings
Black Royal Icing
cardboard
beef skewer
wire and black insulation tape

This cake was baked in the microwave oven in an oval 23cm long pyrex bowl. It took approximately six minutes to cook.

Cover the cake with the Royal Icing thinly spread.

Colour 300gm Fondant Icing, pale blue. Roll out to .5cm thick and an oval shape the length of the bowl plus 5cm in length and width for the sides. Place on the cake.

Roll White Icing out to 1cm thick and cut to a windsurfer shape.

Colour a small amount of Fondant Icing with red powder dye, roll out into small strips and place on the "board" as in the photograph.

Pipe the lines and name with Black Royal Icing and a No. 2 writing nozzle.

Cut white cardboard to a "sail" shape and use gummed paper to acquire the colours of your favourite windsurfer. Gladwrap is placed over the "see-through" section in the sail to make it look authentic.

The wish bone is wire twisted together at the ends, covered with Black Insulation Tape and set in position with two toothpicks pushed through the cardboard. The "sail" is taped to the mast with gummed paper, then pressed into the "board" and through into the cake.

It is possible to purchase swimmers made of metal or plastic from cake decorating shops.

The "waves" are piped with a No. 2 icing nozzle and Buttercream Icing.

Space and Fantasy

CLOWN

1 20cm apple cake round
1 small loaf cake
1 patty pan cake
1½ recipe Yellow Buttercream Icing
400gm Fondant Icing
red powder food colouring
licorice
pebbles

The apple cake forms the face, the loaf cake is cut into the hat and the neck frill, and I used a muffin for the pom-pom.

Join the three cake sections together with jam and whipped cream and smooth a thin layer of Yellow Buttercream Icing all over the top of the cakes.

Roll out some White Fondant Icing to .5cm thick and 19cm in diameter and place over the clown's face.

Pipe stars, hair and frills with Yellow Buttercream Icing and use a star icing nozzle. Anchor licorice to earrings, pebbles on the hat, and cut small strips of licorice for the eyes and eyebrows.

Colour a fist full of Fondant Icing with red food powder a few days earlier if possible to bring out a true red colour, and shape a nose and a mouth. Rub a little red dye into the cheeks for a good clown 'look'.

CIRCUS

1 20cm round apple cake
½ recipe of Yellow Buttercream
  Icing
200gm Red Fondant Icing
black powder food colouring
cigarette sweets
pebbles
sugar crystals
4 elephants
1 clown
1 candy windmill

Roll out the Red Fondant Icing to .5cm thick, 7cm wide and as long as the circumference of the cake.

Smooth a thin layer of Yellow Buttercream Icing over the top and sides of the cake, and press the Red Fondant Icing strip onto the side of the cake.

Pipe a scroll of Yellow Buttercream Icing around the base of the Red Fondant Icing with a star icing nozzle and press pebbles into position. The cigarettes are anchored with a dot of Buttercream Icing half way up the Red Fondant Icing.

Fill the 'arena' with sugar crystals. Anchor all the toys with a dot of Buttercream Icing.

Colour some Fondant Icing Black and use for modelling a stool and seal.

FLYING SAUCER

1 pkt of cake mix
400gm Pink Fondant Icing
500gm Pink Buttercream Icing
pebbles
oddfellows
licorice staples
candles
tinsel
pink pipe cleaners

This cake was baked in the microwave in a glass bowl for six minutes, inverted, cooled then iced thinly with Pink Buttercream Icing.

Roll out the Pink Fondant Icing to form a circle and mould this carefully over the dome of the cake and cut away excess icing.

Pipe scrolls and stars with a star icing nozzle and Pink Buttercream Icing. Pipe lines with a No. 2 icing nozzle.

Press all sweets and candles into position in the photograph.

Make a circle with the tinsel and bend the pipe cleaner onto the connection. Press the pipe cleaner into the cake.

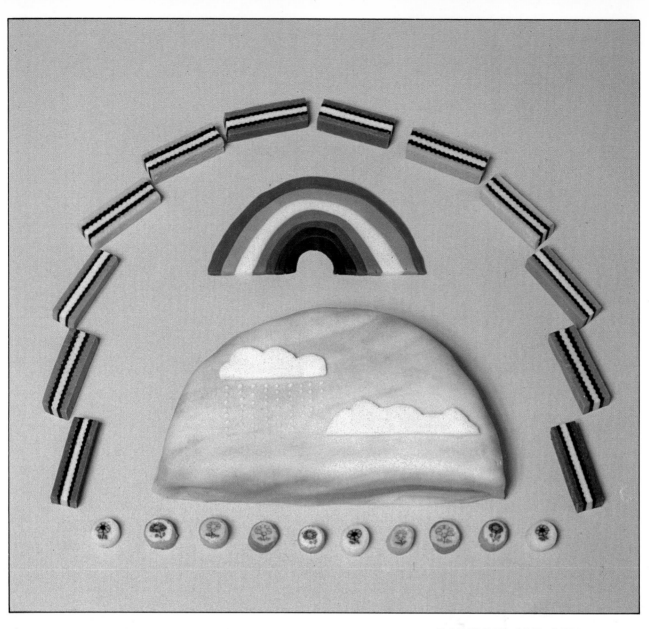

RAINBOW AND SKY

1 20cm round apple cake
500gm Fondant Icing
boiled sweets
licorice allsorts
assorted food colourings

This tends to look more like a photographer's artwork than a cake but it is colourful and fun!

The round cake is cut in half and one half is set into the other with jam and whipped cream between the layers and a little jam on top.

The marbled sky effect is achieved by half kneading the blue food colouring into the Fondant Icing. The 'sky' is rolled out to .5cm thick and placed over the cake, trimmed, and the excess Fondant Icing is cut away.

Little clouds are modelled from Fondant Icing and dampened slightly underneath to attach them to the cake.

The rainbow is the result of experimenting with different amounts of dye added to the Fondant Icing and tests one's ability in creating a colour wheel.

The sweets are arranged to create an interesting effect.

SUNSHINE

1 20cm round ice cream cake
1 recipe Buttercream Icing
1 tsp yellow food colouring
15 candy snakes
Black Royal Icing

Microwave approximately two litres of French Vanilla Ice Cream gently then place into a lined 20cm round cake pan and refreeze.

When frozen, turn cake out, remove paper and quickly ice the surface with Yellow Buttercream Icing and pipe the scroll work with a star icing nozzle.

The face can be decorated with licorice but I used a small amount of Black Royal Icing and a No. 2 icing nozzle.

The snake ends are tucked under the cake and one tip is placed in the sun's 'mouth' for its tongue.

This cake can be frozen decorated or eaten straight away.

ROCKET

2 jam sponge rolls
750gm White Fondant Icing
½ recipe of Buttercream Icing
6 candy sticks
1 licorice strap
red star stickers
American flag sticker
cardboard
wooden blocks
beef skewer
royal blue gum paper

Place the sponge rolls end to end and measure. Next measure the circumference of one sponge roll.

Roll out the Fondant to these two measurements and spread Buttercream Icing lightly over the whole Fondant surface. Place the cakes on the edge of the Fondant Icing, roll up and a cylinder results.

Cut cardboard approximately 30cm x 7.5cm, cover with silver foil, smear a small amount of jam down the centre of the board and place cylinder on top.

Cut rocket's tail and sidefins as in Diagram B, and press gently into the Fondant. Attach licorice pieces to the rocket with spots of Buttercream Icing.

Cover beef skewer with foil and place into top of rocket and make nose cone from royal blue gum paper see Diagram A, and press lightly into icing.

The candles can be placed directly behind the red stars. Cover wooden blocks or off cuts with silver foil to represent ramps.

Set cake on an angle about one hour before party is ready. Then press candy sticks into tail of rocket, some will need to be broken to achieve correct proportions.

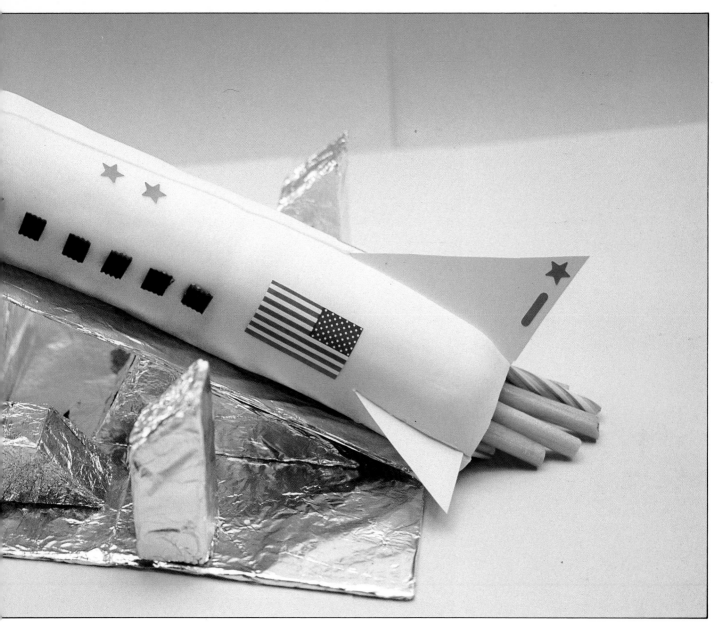

Diagram A Nose Cone

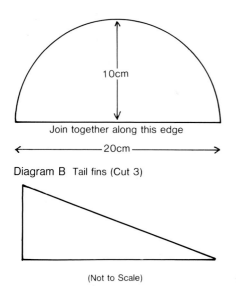

10cm

Join together along this edge

← 20cm →

Diagram B Tail fins (Cut 3)

(Not to Scale)

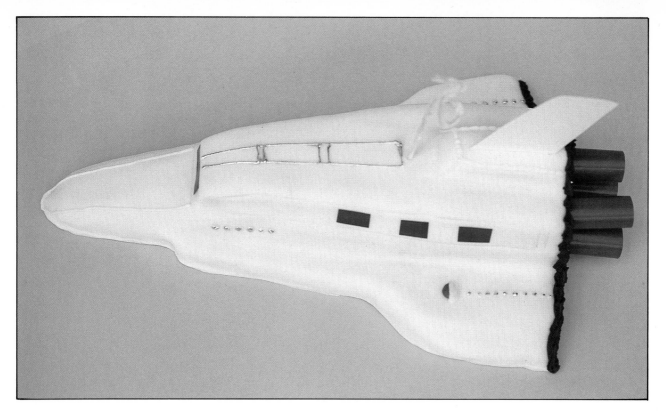

SHUTTLE

1 chocolate cake baked in a swiss
roll tin
1 recipe Royal Icing
500gm Fondant Icing
300ml cream, whipped
blue food colouring (powder form)
2 small red sweets
royal blue gummed paper
white cardboard
non-toxic silver paint
1 white pipe cleaner

Carefully cut the cake referring to Diagram (A). Place sections (i) and (ii) on top of original cake as in diagram (B). Jam and whipped cream are used to connect all pieces. Cut a sloping nose cone and put this extra piece of cake onto the tail fin area. Cover the cake completely with a thin layer of whipped cream.

Roll out the Fondant Icing to .5cm thick and the length and width of the swiss roll tin, plus an extra 8cm added to the width for the Shuttle's rear height. Lay this Fondant Icing shape over the shuttle, gently press into the cake contours and trim away excess Fondant Icing.

Pipe all the features of the shuttle with White Royal Icing and a No. 2 icing nozzle. Attach blue gummed paper for portholes, and cut small cylinders of gummed paper for the rockets. Press these rockets into the rear of the shuttle where Blue Royal Icing has been placed.

With a toothpick touch silver paint over the dots and lines when they are dry. Refer to photograph.

Attach red sweets for "lights". The "aerial" is a twisted pipe cleaner.

Cut out the tail piece from white cardboard using diagram (c), and press this into the Fondant Icing surface.

Diagram A

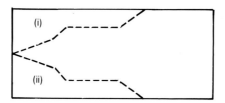

Diagram B
Section (i) and (ii) placed on top of original cake

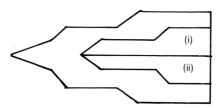

Diagram C Tail fin

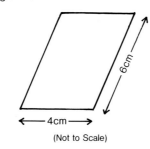

6cm

4cm

(Not to Scale)

SPACEMEN

1 recipe banana cake
**200gm Fondant Icing coloured dark
  brown**
brown sugar crystals
plastic spacemen and models

This is a very simple and yet effective
cake. Basically any shaped cake can be
used.

Ice the cake roughly with the
Buttercream Icing to give a "textured"
finish.

Model the Dark Brown Fondant Icing
into "moon rocks".

Situate rocks, spacemen and brown
sugar crystals at random over the cake.

Most cake decorating shops sell
these plastic figures.

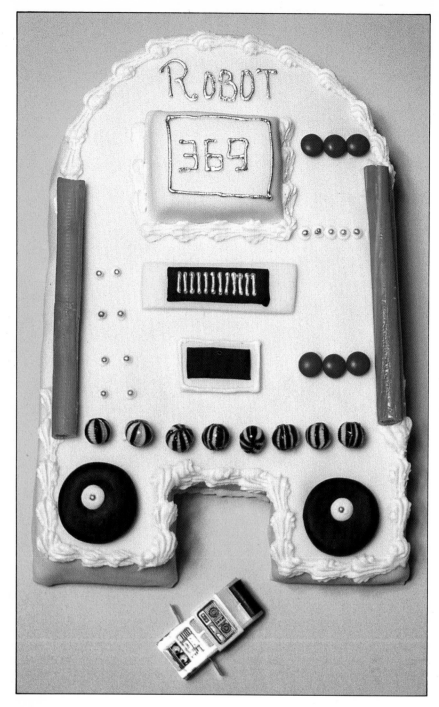

Diagram A   Diagram B

(Not to Scale)

ROBOT

**1 chocolate cake baked in a swiss
   roll tin
500gm Fondant Icing
½ recipe Royal Icing
yellow and black food colourings
8 blackballs
6 red pebbles
2 green candy sticks
Non-toxic silver paint
1 'Robot' rubber**

Cut the cake as in diagrams (A) and (B),
and place section (i) onto the cake with
jam or whipped cream. Cover cake with
a thin layer of whipped cream.

Roll out the Fondant Icing to .5cm
thick and the width plus 5cm and
breadth plus 5cm of a swiss roll tin.
Carefully place this shape onto the cake
moulding with your hands to achieve
neatened sides. Cut out and add an
extra piece of Fondant Icing to the area
between the robot's feet.

Pipe White Royal Icing with a star
icing nozzle where all scroll work occurs
on the cake. A No. 2 icing nozzle will
pipe the lines and numbers and attach
all the sweets.

Colour some Fondant Icing yellow and
cut out two oblong pieces as in the
photograph.

Colour some Fondant Icing black for
the "wheels" and two oblong pieces.

With a toothpick touch all dots and
lines with non-toxic silver paint where
they occur in the photograph.

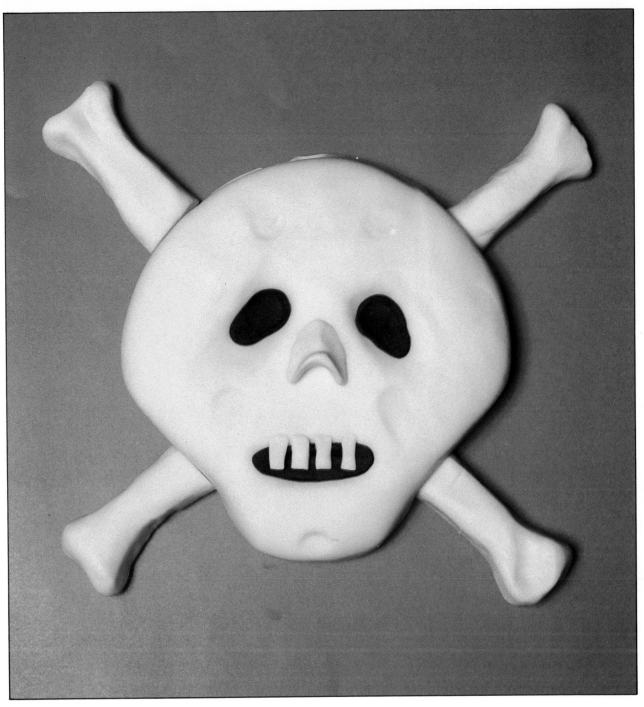

Diagram A

Cut out (i) and
(ii) sections

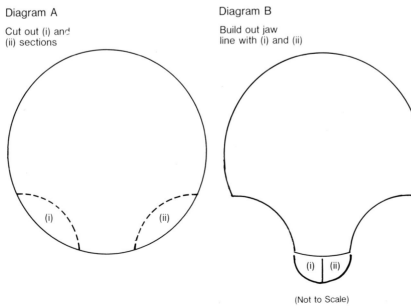

(i) (ii)

Diagram B

Build out jaw
line with (i) and (ii)

(i) | (ii)

(Not to Scale)

SKULL

1 20cm round sponge cake
500gm Cream Fondant Icing
black powdered food colouring

Trim the cake as in diagrams (A) and (B).
Join pieces together with jam and
whipped cream.

Model a small amount of Black
Fondant Icing into two eyes and a
mouth.

Roll out the Cream Coloured Fondant
Icing and place carefully over the cake
pressing indentations into jaw,
cheekbones, forehead and model a
small bridge for the nose.

Make "bones" and set into position.
Cut out four "teeth" and attach to mouth
dampening the underside slightly to get
good adhering properties.

The bones could also be placed
crossed beneath the skull in traditional
pirate's flag manner!

BLUE MONSTER
1 20cm round apple cake
1 recipe Buttercream Icing
250gm Fondant Icing
red, blue and black powdered food
colourings

Colour 100gm of Fondant Icing with
blue powder food colouring. Colour
100gm of Fondant Icing red and a small
amount of icing colour black for the eye
pupils. Model the nose, horns, mouth,
teeth and eyes from these coloured
Fondant Icings.

With a star icing nozzle and an icing
bag, swirl the "hair" of the monster all
over the round cake. Set the face
features into the cake as shown in the
photograph.

Pipe the monsters 'moustache' last of
all.

PEPPERMINT MONSTER

**1 chocolate cake baked in a swiss
    roll tin
500gm Chocolate Buttercream Icing
300gm White Fondant Icing
black powdered food colouring
1 pkt small peppermints**

Cut the cake as for Hickory Dickory Dock shape, and use the top cut out pieces for the "whiskers" at the base of the monster's head.

Smooth Chocolate Buttercream Icing all over the cake, then fill an icing bag with the remaining Buttercream and place a star icing nozzle on the bag.

With White Fondant Icing model the whites of the eyes and several fangs for the mouth.

Model a nose from Black Fondant Icing pressing two depressions for nostrils in a small ball of the Fondant. Model two black ears and a flat strip for the mouth.

Hold the icing bag and swirl the monster's hair around the face accentuating eyebrows and whiskers.

Press in all the facial features, then the peppermints.

Boys and Girls

SANDCASTLE

1 pkt cake mix
100gm Fondant Icing
1 recipe Buttercream plus 1tbs
  cocoa
3 jube snakes
pebbles
licorice
bubblegum strips

Place the cake mixture into a child's bucket and bake approximately six minutes in the microwave oven. Test with a toothpick. Turn out carefully and cool.

Ice the side and top of the cake marking out the castellations. Set pieces of licorice into the cake to form windows and door as in the photograph.

Press pebbles round the base of the cake. Cut bubblegum strip diagonally and stand up on top of the cake.

Model shells by pressing slightly cocoa-coloured Fondant Icing against real shells to acquire the markings.

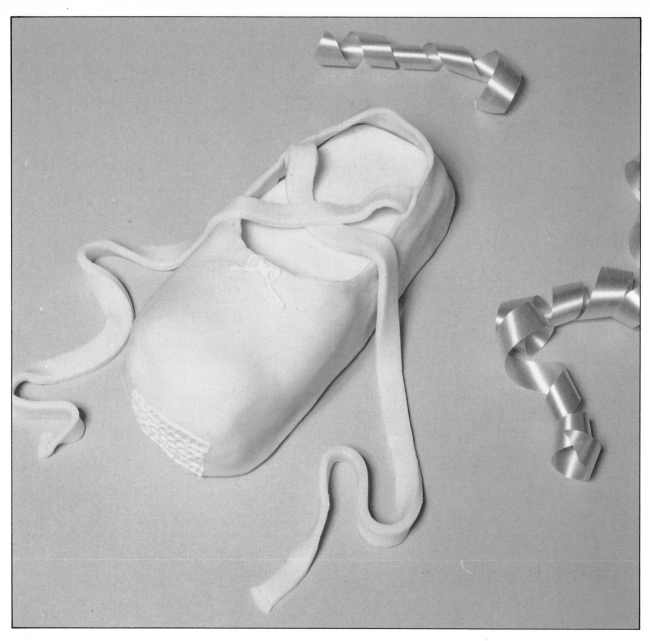

BALLET SHOE

1 loaf cake
500gm Pale Pink Fondant Icing
1 drop of yellow food colouring
2tbs Pink Royal Icing
½ recipe Pink Buttercream Icing

Knead the yellow drop of food colouring into the Pink Fondant Icing to create the special ballet shoe colour rather than the blue-pink of ordinary colouring.

To create the sole of the shoe slice across the top of the loaf 2.5cm thick and place this piece of cake onto the toe piece.

Smooth the Pink Buttercream Icing all over the cake creating rounded edges as on a real ballet shoe.

Roll out the Pink Fondant Icing to .5cm thick and cut a "sole" placing this over the shoe first and run the piece up to the bow of the toe section. Cut two strips 1.5cm wide and 45cm long.

Reroll the remaining Fondant Icing to .75cm thick and carefully mould the toe piece and side sections of the shoe. The sides of the shoe should stand up. Bunched up tissue paper inside the shoe will support the sides for an hour or so.

Press dampened ends of straps to the shoe sides, cross over and drape decoratively.

With Pink Royal Icing and a No. 2 icing nozzle, pipe "embroidery" on toe piece and the little bow.

Diagram A

BALLET STAGE

**1 20cm diam. rounded sponge cake
1 20cm x 11cm loaf sponge cake
1 recipe of Buttercream Icing
300gm Pink Fondant Icing
cachous
pink curling ribbon
4 ballet dancers
2 sprigs of Lily of the Valley**

Slice cakes as in diagram (A) and set in position as in diagram (B).

Ice the stage thickly and smoothly with the Buttercream Icing, and ice the backdrop thinly. Press approximately 40cm of wide lace around the stage.

Roll out the Pink Fondant Icing to a semi-circle and .5cm thick and press onto the backdrop, moulding carefully over the top.

Pipe stars over the lace with a star icing nozzle and Buttercream Icing, then set a cachou into each star. Pipe sweeping strands at either side of backdrop to "gather" up for curtains. Pipe four stars on the stage and position the dancers.

Place curling ribbon and Lily of the Valley into position on the top of the cake. Two small ribbon bows are set into the curtains for "ties".

The little ballet shoes are modelled from the remaining Pink Fondant Icing from the backstage.

(i)

- - - - - - - - - -

(ii)

(iii)

Loaf cake

Diagram B

(i)

(iii) Loaf cake

(ii)

(Not to Scale)

BUCKET AND SPADE
1 pkt cake mix
500gm Red Fondant Icing
100gm marzipan
1 small strip of White Fondant
½ recipe of Buttercream Icing
brown sugar crystals

Place the cake mix into a cleaned child's bucket and bake approximately six minutes in the microwave. Test with a toothpick. Turn out carefully and cool.

Roll out the Fondant Icing to .75cm thick and into a rectangular shape as long as the bucket's circumference and as wide as the bucket's height.

Ice the "top" and sides of the cake with the Buttercream Icing.

Place the iced cake sideways onto the rectangle and carefully roll up to make the sides of the bucket. Seal the edges by pressing together and smoothing.

Attach the Fondant Icing strip to either side of the bucket for the "handles".

Model a spade from the marzipan. Mix equal quantities of Red Fondant Icing and marzipan together to form the orange colour to make the crab.

PINE CONE

1 20cm round chocolate cake
1 recipe Chocolate Buttercream
Icing plus 3tbs cream
2 small pkts chocolate buttons
licorice

Prepare soft Buttercream Icing by adding the 3 tbs cream beating it into the mixture.

Cut the sides off the cake as in the diagram and pile (i) and (ii) sections on top of the cake making one end higher than the other. Adhere all pieces together with jam and whipped cream then ice over completely with Chocolate Buttercream Icing.

Work quickly and press the chocolate buttons into the Buttercream overlapping each other and beginning with the top of the cone.

All the chocolate swirls on the buttons should point down as in a real pine cone.

Place licorice in the higher end of the cake for the stalk.

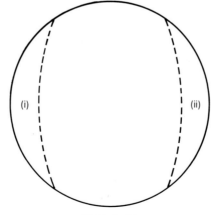

(i)   (ii)

(Not to Scale)

SUN FLOWER

1 20cm round sponge cake
1 recipe Yellow Buttercream Icing
300gm White Fondant Icing
yellow liquid food colouring
green leaf sweets
1 dragon fly & 2 bees
Black Royal Icing
yellow sweets

Place whipped cream and jam inside the cake, then cover the top and sides completely with the Yellow Buttercream Icing. With a star-shaped icing nozzle pipe scrolls on the top and bottom edges of the cake.

Roll out the White Fondant Icing to .75cm thick. Shape a round sunflower by cutting around the tin. Press a glass rim into the centre of the cake to get the outline of the face then "radiate" petal lines with a knife edge.

Trim the petals into points. Paint yellow food colouring onto the tips of the petal edges. Attach the yellow sweets with a small amount of Buttercream Icing. With Black Royal icing and a No. 2 icing nozzle pipe the face.

Carefully place this flower and face onto the cake.

Attach bees, dragonfly and leaf sweets.

SPA POOL

1 20cm round chocolate cake
1 recipe of Chocolate Buttercream
   Icing
500gm Fondant Icing
colourings — blue, brown, pink,
   black, red
100gm marzipan
plastic bottle
sprigs of rosemary
cotton wool
Royal Icing

This is a fun cake to make for a pool party, and if you are extra clever the people can be modelled like some of your eccentric friends! A lot of coloured fondant and modelling expertise are needed in this piece of artwork!

Cover the cake with Chocolate Buttercream Icing. Colour Fondant pale blue and roll out into a small circle and place in the centre of the cake. This circle may be covered with a small amount of gladwrap to give an authentic "water" look.

Colour approximately 300gm of Fondant Icing brown and roll out to

.75cm thick, cut a hole for the spa, place over the cake and mark out "bricks" with a knife edge.

Model a towel and slippers from the marzipan and Blue Fondant Icing. Model people and feet and set onto the spa pool.

The people's features are piped with coloured Royal Icing and a No. 2 icing nozzle.

From brown Fondant Icing model tubs and press small rosemary sprigs into the tubs for "trees".

Cotton wool can be added to represent "steam".

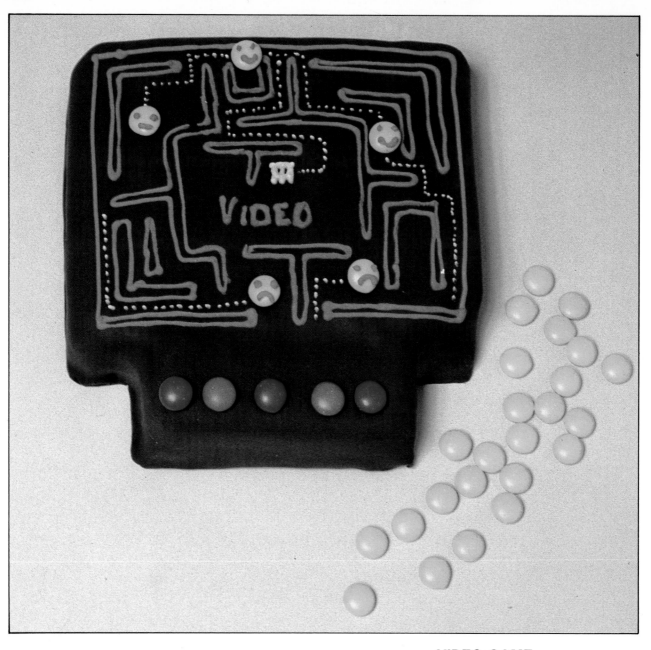

VIDEO GAME

1 25cm square banana cake
½ recipe Buttercream Icing
400gm Black Fondant Icing
Royal Icing — white and blue
red and yellow sweets

Prepare the Black Fondant Icing 3 days beforehand to achieve an intense colour. Add one tsp of black powdered food colouring and knead in well. Kneading occasionally over the three days.

Cut two corners out of the square cake. These could make a "joystick" by joining together with jam and whipped cream, then covering with left over Black Fondant Icing and a piece of licorice for the "stick".

Smooth the Buttercream Icing over the cake. Roll out the Black Fondant Icing to .5cm thick and carefully mould over the cake.

Pipe the blue lines, faces, white dots and ghosts with the Royal Icings and a No. 2 icing nozzle.

Attach the sweets to the cake with dots of Royal Icing.

GOLDEN DOLL CAKE

1 pkt cake mix
1 recipe of plain Buttercream Icing
400gm Pale Yellow Fondant Icing or
**   Marzipan**
boiled sweets
orange and lemon jubes
cachous
1 doll approximately 20cm tall.

The cake is baked in a Dolly Varden tin which has been carefully greased and floured. Turn out the cooked cake and cool.

Cut out a hole in the top of the cake as for the Red Riding Hood cake.

Smooth Buttercream Icing onto the surface of the cake. Roll out the Fondant Icing to .5cm thick and to the measurements in the diagram.

Carefully mould this "skirt" over the cake, sealing the slightly dampened edges of the skirt down the back of the dress.

Mould the bodice of the dress with more Fondant Icing and make a bow and two sashes for the back to cover the seal of the skirt.

Fill an icing bag with Buttercream, and using a star nozzle pipe all the sweets into position beginning at the hem. The "buttons" are stars with a cachou in the centre. The hat is piped straight onto the hair and a boiled sweet placed on top.

←14cm→   ←14cm→
23cm
14cm
70cm

(Not to Scale)

57

MOTOR MOWER

1 chocolate cake baked in a swiss roll tin
500gm Fondant Icing
½ recipe Buttercream Icing
½ tsp green powder food colouring
1 tsp black powder food colouring
1 red pebble
4 shrewsberry biscuits
3 beef skewers
silver non-toxic paint

Cut 6cm off down the length of the cake as in diagram A. Carefully slice the rest of the cake through transversely. Round the ends on the bottom piece as for a mower, slide the top piece back 13cm and cut 13cm off the end. This end piece is placed on top to form the "catcher". The side piece of cake (i) is also cut to shape the "catcher" and make the engine box section (ii).

Cover the whole mower thinly with Buttercream Icing.

Colour 300gm of the Fondant with the black powder three days beforehand if possible to give a good deep colour. Roll this out to .5cm thick and mould around the "catcher" the wheel tyres, engine and parts and wheel "hubs". Make good tyre tracks with a knife edge.

Colour approximately 200 gms of the Fondant Icing with the green food powder, roll out and carefully place over the mower, cutting all sections as on the photograph.

Attach wheels with Buttercream Icing. Petrol "lid" is the red pebble and is also attached with this icing. Pipe with a No. 2 icing nozzle the "Mower" and the "M".

The handle is made of foil covered beefskewers cut and taped together and pressed on an angle into the cake. Where the hole shows as the handle enters the cake cover with a small piece of Fondant Icing and two dots to form "nails". The nails are painted with the silver non-toxic paint.

Diagram A

(i)

6cm

(ii)

Diagram B Top view

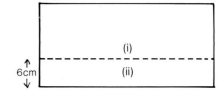

(ii)

Diagram C Side view

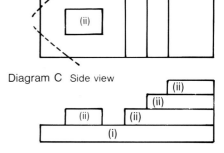

(ii)
(ii)
(ii) (ii)
(i)

(Not to Scale)

TRAIN

2 x 20cm square cakes
2 recipes Buttercream Icing
jam and cream for filling
green, brown, pink and black food
** colourings**
1 pkt chocolate fingers
assorted sweets: black jubes for
** wheels**
licorice
pebbles
200gm Fondant Icing
yellow banana sweets
toothpicks
6 animal biscuits
plastic clown head
100gm castor sugar

Cut the first cake into 4 pieces all 10cm x 7.5cm. These will make four carriages. The second cake will cut into a long train, one more carriage, and the remaining cake will form the top section of the train.

Cream and jam all the carriages.

Smooth Buttercream Icing over the train and 2 carriages.

Colour some Buttercream brown and smooth this over 2 more carriages. Colour the remaining carriage with Buttercream Icing coloured green.

Press chocolate fingers into the carriages as in the photograph. Press black jubes in for wheels. Fill the carriages with the sweets and biscuits.

Colour the castor sugar with 3 drops of pink food colouring in a cup and stir well with a small spoon.

With a star icing nozzle, a bag and Green Buttercream Icing, pipe "stars" in the centre of each wheel.

Colour the Fondant Icing 3 days beforehand with a small amount of black powdered colouring and knead well over the next 3 days. Roll the Fondant out to .5cm thick, and lay over the train, carefully pressing in at the corners. Cut away excess icing with a small sharp knife. Model a "seat" for the clown. Press clown into the seat. Press pebbles into the front of the train. Place more pebbles in the "funnels" made with toothpicks.

Press licorice into the train and carriages for the windows and connecting "rods".

Numbers

NUMBER ONE

**1 loaf cake of any recipe or No. 1 tin
1 recipe of plain Buttercream Icing
licorice staples**

This simple and effective cake is decorated with Buttercream Icing smoothed on with a knife, then licorice staples are carefully set in lines down the cake.

Make sure the Buttercream Icing is soft on the cake. Do not leave it any longer than half an hour or the sweets will not adhere securely.

Any of the following numbers can be decorated this way and conversely.

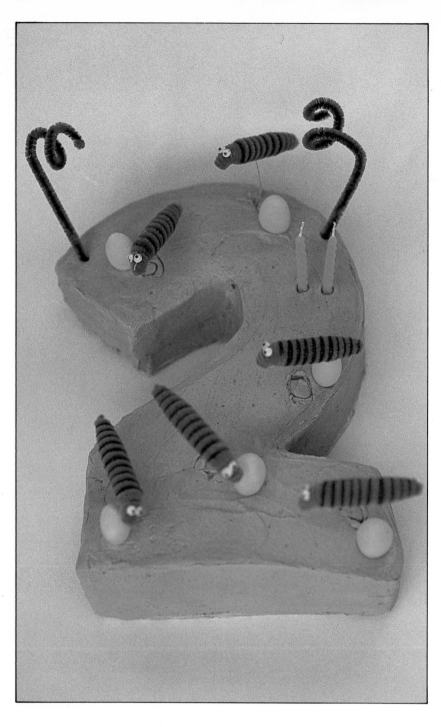

NUMBER TWO

**1 cake mix recipe or chocolate cake
recipe**
No. 2 tin shape
**1 recipe of Buttercream Icing plus
1tsp liquid green food colouring**
6 green furry caterpillars
6 green coated almonds
2 green pipe cleaners
2 green candles

This fun cake would be good to give to
your favourite gardener! The caterpillars
are obtainable from cake decorating
shops and pet shops and gardening
supplies?

The No. 2 tin can be hired or
purchased from cake decorating shops.
It should be well greased and floured
before the cake is cooked in it.

When the cake is cool, cover
completely with the Green Buttercream
Icing and use a warmed knife to achieve
a smooth finish.

Press the caterpillars into the cake on
cute angles. Also press in the almonds,
candles and pipe cleaners.

NUMBER THREE

1 pkt cake mix or 1 chocolate cake
   recipe
No. 3 tin shape
1 recipe Buttercream Icing plus 1tsp
   yellow liquid food colouring
yellow pebbles
1 pkt lemon or orange slices
gold leaves
3 yellow candles

Thoroughly grease and flour the No. 3 tin. When cooked, carefully turn out onto a cake rack.

Cut the lemon and orange slices in half to form the flower petals as in the photograph.

When the cake is cool, completely cover it with the Yellow Buttercream Icing and press all the sweets, leaves and candles into the cake as in the photograph.

NUMBER FOUR

1 pkt cake mix or 1 chocolate cake
    recipe
No. 4 tin shape
1 recipe Chocolate Buttercream
    Icing
400gm White Fondant Icing
blue, green, black food colourings
coconut coloured green
4 red candles
1 plastic fisherman
sprigs of rosemary

The ideas for this cake come from men's birthdays whose hobbies are fishing, hunting, tramping, camping or shooting.

The No. 4 tin has no allowance for the hole in the centre — the lake compensates here!

Colour the coconut, model all the trees, tent and rocks before the Buttercream Icing is put onto the cake.

The icing has better adhering qualities when it is newly put on the cake's surface.

From 100gm of Fondant Icing model a tent. Add a small amount of black colouring powder to another 100gm of Fondant and model several rocks.

The trees are made from 100gm of Fondant Icing with ½tsp green powdered food colouring and 2 drops of green liquid colouring kneaded together

well. Shape four cones and with the tops of scissors, clip the "branches" of the trees into shape beginning at the bottom. This gives a very effective result. Store all these models on waxed paper in an airy place — not the refrigerator. They will harden in a short time.

The other 100gm of Fondant Icing is coloured pale blue and kept in plastic until ready to be made into a "lake" and placed on the cake.

Cover the cake with the chocolate Buttercream Icing. Press in all rocks, grass, trees and tent.

Quickly shape the lake and press into position.

With a No. 2 icing nozzle pipe bodies and heads of ducks on the lake. With a star nozzle pipe a scroll around the top edge of the cake.

NUMBER FIVE

1 chocolate cake recipe
No. 5 tin shape
1 recipe of Chocolate Buttercream
    Icing
100gm Fondant Icing
2 pkts chocolate flake
Black Royal Icing
2 plastic trees
1 witch
1 frog

This cake could be used for Halloween Night!

Make sure the tin is carefully greased and floured before the cake mixture is placed in it.

The Chocolate Buttercream Icing is smoothed carefully over the cake with a warmed knife to achieve a good surface. Push the chocolate flake "logs" into position. Add the trees, witch and frog.

The "ghosts" are made from golf-ball-sized pieces of fondant with little skirts modelled at the bottom. Very easily they are created into "ghosts" by piping Black Royal Icing "faces" onto the shapes with a No. 2 icing nozzle. These ghosts can also be used for Video Games cakes.

NUMBER SIX

1 pkt cake mix
No. 6 tin shape (or No. 9)
1 recipe Pale Pink Buttercream Icing
300gms Pale Pink Fondant Icing
3 pink dolls
1 pkt marshallows
ribbon
Lily of the Valley
pink candles

Little dolls, heart-shaped objects, marshmallows and the colour pink are my daughter's greatest delights. Imagine the effect of this cake on her little face!

Roll out the Fondant Icing to .5cm thick and use the tin to cut out the "6" shape.

Smooth the Buttercream Icing all over the cake's surface and sides. Place the fondant shape carefully on the top, and smooth with your hand. Press marshmallows into the sides.

Fill a bag with the Buttercream Icing and with a star icing nozzle pipe "stars" all around the top edge of the cake, the circle in the centre between the marshmallows, and for the bases of the candles.

Ribbon is tied onto and around the Lily of the Valley and set into the Buttercream stars. Set in the candles and the dolls.

The dolls, purchased from cake decorating shops, have pegs on them to anchor into the cake.

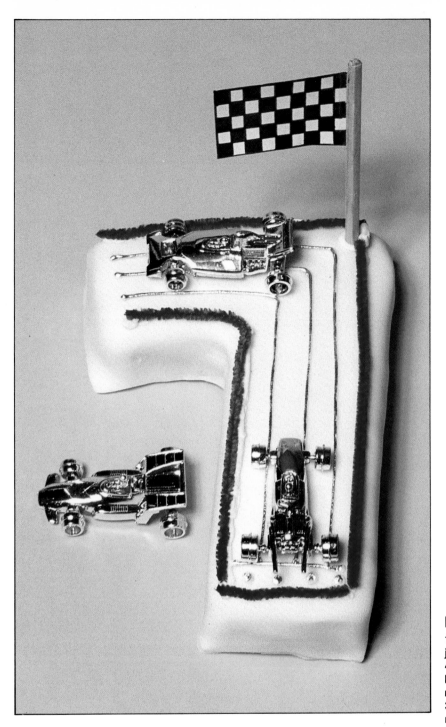

NUMBER SEVEN

1 chocolate cake recipe
jam and cream
400gm Fondant Icing
Royal Icing
red pipe cleaners
3 racing cars
non-toxic silver paint
Dowling and cardboard

The chocolate cake is baked in two small loaf tins, shaped together and trimmed to create the No. "7".

Fill the cake with jam and cream and smooth some cream over the top and sides of the cake.

Roll out the Fondant Icing to .75cm thick and carefully shape over the cake, taking most care over the innermost corner of the No. "7".

With Royal Icing and a No. 2 icing nozzle pipe the "tracks" and "starting line" and adhere the cut pipe cleaners to the outer lines.

To make the flag cut the cardboard to 7cm x 5cm and mark the squares with a felt tip pen. Sellotape this to a piece of dowling 10cm long.

When the "tracks" are dry, with a toothpick paint on the non-toxic silver paint.

NUMBER EIGHT

1 20cm round banana cake
1 25cm round chocolate cake
1 recipe Yellow Buttercream Icing
300ml cream
hundreds and thousands
pebbles
one bunch of plastic balloons

This cake when cut can be offered as either chocolate or banana!

Trim off a small piece from each round cake and fit the flat ends together with jam.

Smooth all over with Yellow Buttercream Icing and press the pebbles all round the base of the cakes.

With a star icing nozzle pipe a scroll around the top edge of the No. "8".

The balloons are joined together and have one spike which is easily pressed into the cake.

At the last moment before the party whip the cream and pipe the large swirls around the two circles. Sprinkle with the hundreds and thousands last of all. If done too soon the colour will "run" from the hundreds and thousands and the effect will become dulled.

Diagram A

Diagram B

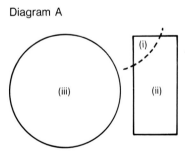

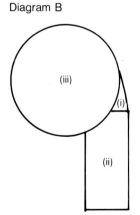

NUMBER NINE

3 litres of ice-cream or
1 chocolate cake recipe
1 recipe Buttercream Icing
300gm Fondant Icing
blue food colouring
2 black jelly babies
33 coloured eskimos

EITHER: Melt gently the three litres of ice-cream and place into fully lined round and loaf tins and refreeze.

OR: Bake the chocolate cake recipe in an 18cm round tin and a loaf tin.

There is a No. "9" tin shape available in cake decorating shops.

Trim the loaf and round cakes as in the diagrams.

Cover completely with the Buttercream Icing. Colour some Fondant Icing blue and roll out to .5cm thick and cut to the size of the cake. Working quickly, lay this on the cake's surface.

Fill a bag with Buttercream Icing and using a star icing nozzle pipe a scroll around the top edge of the cake, press the eskimos into this. Pipe "waves" and attach the other eskimo and two jelly babies onto the Fondant Icing.

Model an igloo from Fondant Icing and with a knife press in the "blocks of ice".

The other seals and walrus are in the photograph to give an Arctic "look"!

Refreeze the cake if it is the ice-cream cake.

Animals

7

BUMBLE BEE

1 20cm round banana cake
1 recipe Yellow Buttercream Icing
400gm Fondant Icing
1tsp black powdered food colouring
1 licorice strap
80cm piece of wire
gladwrap
3 bees

Make the Black Fondant Icing 3 days before use and kneading several times to get a true black. Roll a circle of White Fondant Icing and cut a flower shape. Reserve some white for eyes.

Cut the round cake as in diagram (A), sections (i) through to (vi) are added to the tail, and top of the cake for a good bee shape!

Join all the cake together with jam, and smooth the Buttercream neatly over the bee.

Roll the Black Fondant Icing to .5cm thick and cut 2 strips 4cm wide to press into the abdomen. The "stinger" is modelled by creating a cap-shape of icing and drawing the sting out and up into a point with the fingertips.

Make licorice feelers, legs, face and eyes. Flatten 2 small balls of White Fondant Icing to make eyes. Press all these features into the bee cake.

The wings are each a piece of 40cm long wire bent onto itself and twisted round as in diagram (B). Wrap gladwrap over the wire — it will attach to itself very efficiently. Pipe "veins" of the wing and the centre dots of the flower with a No. 2 icing nozzle and Yellow Buttercream icing

Diagram A

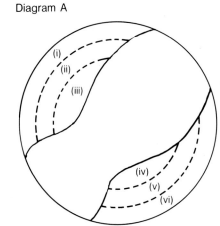

Diagram B

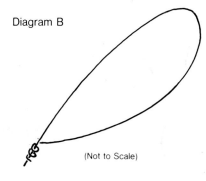

(Not to Scale)

PORCUPINE

1 chocolate cake recipe baked in a swiss roll tin
1 recipe of Chocolate Buttercream Icing
2 licorice straps
a pair of plastic eyes
jam and cream
Black Fondant Icing or black wine gum

Cut the cake to the shape in the diagram. Cream and jam the top of section (v) then pile up the other four sections to make a high round body.

Smooth the chocolate Buttercream all over the body and shape down to a point at the nose.

Cut the licorice straps into narrow 2.5cm strips and press these into the porcupine for spines.

Press the eyes into position.

Model a "nose" with 2 "nostrils" for the porcupine out of Black Fondant Icing (see the notes on Fondant at beginning of the book).

A black wine gum could make a suitable nose.

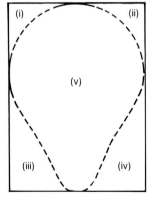

(Not to Scale)

RABBIT

1 double rabbit tin
1 recipe of chocolate cake
1½ recipe of Buttercream Icing
blue and pink food colouring
white pipe cleaners
marshmallows
blue ribbon
licorice
Fondant Icing
coconut

This tin can be purchased or hired from a few cake decorating shops.

Grease and flour the tin thoroughly. Place the cake mixture in the "face" tin and place the "back" tin over the top. Tape together securely with cloth tape making sure the air hole is not covered. Bake approximately 45 minutes. A small amount of cake may 'dribble' through the air hole and this shows the cake has filled both pans on expansion.

When cooked, open the tin carefully and turn out onto a wire rack.

Make the eyes with flattened balls of Pale Pink Fondant Icing pressed onto flattened balls of White Fondant Icing. Dot with licorice for the irises of the eyes. Licorice placed under two ovals of Fondant Icing forms the mouth.

Sit the Rabbit cake vertically and anchor in place with jam. Smooth Buttercream Icing over the "tail" and inner "ears". Colour the rest of the icing pale blue and smooth all over the rabbit with a small warmed knife.

Press the blue bow, pipe cleaners for whiskers, eyes and mouth into position.

White marshmallows and coconut are spread around the cake.

Diagram A

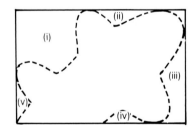

Diagram B

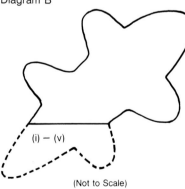

(i) – (v)

(Not to Scale)

CROCODILE

**1 chocolate cake baked in a swiss
roll tin
2 recipes Buttercream Icing
1 recipe Royal Icing
2tsp green powdered food colouring
White Fondant Icing
licorice pieces
pebbles for "food crumbs"
blue colouring**

Cut the cake as in diagram (A) and join all
pieces together as in diagram (B) using
the sections to create the long tail, back
right leg and give height to the
backbone.

Make the Green Royal Icing two to
three days beforehand to develop a
good colour add some blue colouring to
give depth of colour.

Cover the cake thinly with
Buttercream Icing. Combine the
remaining Buttercream Icing and the
Green Royal Icing and beat well. Fill an
icing bag with this mixture and using a
star icing nozzle pipe stars and swirls
onto the crocodile to look like scales
and spines.

Teeth, feet and eye whites are
modelled from White Fondant Icing,
press these into position. Make both
upper and lower teeth. Cut licorice into
small round pieces for the eyes and
nostrils.

The pebbles lying around the mouth
represent "crumbs" of food!

PANDA

2 20cm round chocolate cakes
600gm Fondant Icing
1 recipe Buttercream Icing
1tsp black powdered food colouring
2 plastic "eyes"
Black Royal Icing
**orange or any available coloured
ribbon**

Cut the cakes as in diagram (A) and join together with Buttercream Icing as in diagram (B). Smooth Buttercream Icing over the entire surface of the cake.

Roll out 450gm of Fondant Icing to .5cm thick and carefully place it over the cakes excluding the "paws".

Colour 150gms of Fondant Icing with the black powder kneading well. This could be done three days earlier to develop a good intense colour.

Roll out the Black Fondant to .5cm thick and cut four shapes for the legs and mould each one around the leg or paw carefully. Shape a nose and two slightly irregular circles for the eye patches. Mould the remaining Fondant Icing into two ears.

Press the plastic eyes into the circles.

With Black Royal Icing and a No. 2 icing nozzle pipe all the other body features and a line around the neck for the ribbon to adhere to.

Place ribbon over the neck line. Shape a bow and set in place with icing or a pin if necessary.

Diagram A

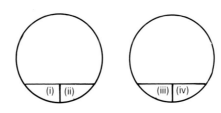

Diagram B

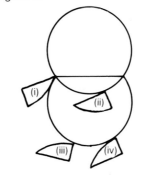

(Not to Scale)

HORSE

1 horseshaped tin
1 chocolate cake recipe
500gm Brown Fondant Icing
1 recipe Chocolate Buttercream Icing
black powdered food colouring

This tin was hired from a cake decorating shop and made everything very much easier.

Grease and flour the tin well to make a clear outline for this cake.

Smooth a thin layer of Chocolate Buttercream Icing over the horse's head and neck.

Roll out the Brown Fondant Icing to .5cm thick, lift onto a rolling pin and drape over the cake, moulding all the features and cutting away the excess icing with a sharp knife.

Depress the nostril with a forefinger, shape the mouth with a knife edge, depress the inner ear and cut a small piece of Fondant Icing for the eye and eyelid.

Colour a portion of Fondant Icing a darker brown with the black powder, roll this out and cut lengths of 2cm wide for the straps and a small ball for the eye.

With Chocolate Buttercream Icing and a star icing nozzle, pipe the horse's mane.

Use your imagination and colour the Fondant according to the colours of your favourite horse!

ELEPHANT

1 20cm round apple cake
1 20cm square apple cake
1 recipe Buttercream Icing
500gm Grey Fondant Icing
White Fondant Icing — eyes and
    tusks
Black Fondant Icing — eyebrows
    and eyes

Cut the two cakes as in diagram (A) and
join together with Buttercream Icing as
in diagram (B).

Colour black 50gm of the 500gm of
Fondant Icing one week before the cake
is constructed. This is to stop the
"flecking" which sometimes occurs in
grey because the dye pigments are not
fully developed and kneaded into the
icing.

Cover the whole cake with the
Buttercream Icing making the outer
ears stand up a little for effect. Extra
Buttercream Icing will be necessary
around the trunk to achieve a good
curve.

Roll out the Grey Fondant Icing and
cut two semicircles. Lie each of these
over the ears and cut away excess icing
with a small knife. Roll out the remaining
icing to .5cm thick and with a rolling pin,
carefully lie the fondant over the head
and trunk. Cut away excess icing, and
with a sharp knife press in "wrinkles"
onto the "trunk".

Model tusks and eyes and eyebrows
with the Black and White Fondant
Icings. Insert tusks into "a socket"
made with extra Grey Fondant Icing.

Diagram A

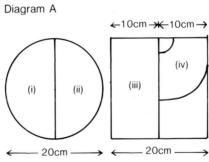

Diagram B

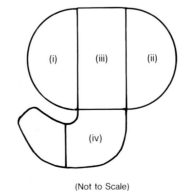

(Not to Scale)

BUTTERFLY

1 20cm round sultana cake
1½ recipes of Yellow Buttercream
Icing
2 licorice straps
lemon and orange slices
bubblegum "money"
blackballs
licorice "chain"
red and yellow pebbles

Cut the round cake in half and press the two rounded edges together in the middle as in the photograph. Cut out small indentations in the flat sides of the wings to create four wings.

Cover the whole butterfly smoothly with Yellow Buttercream Icing.

Cut the licorice into thin strips and press them into the outlines, antennae and dots on the cake.

Press all the other sweets into the Buttercream Icing. The licorice "chain" makes the body section and tail. The antennae are curled around on the cake board.

Endless varieties of shapes, patterns and sweets can be used for this cake.

LADYBIRD

1 25cm round chocolate cake
1 cup cake (chocolate mixture)
400gm Red Fondant Icing
200gm Black Fondant Icing
licorice strap and twists
1 recipe plain Buttercream Icing
brown sweets

The cake is cooked with the cupcake which uses the same mixture.

The two coloured Fondant Icings should be coloured and kneaded three days before the cake is constructed.

Fill the cakes with jam and cream and join the cupcake to the cake with jam. Cover the whole cake with Buttercream Icing.

Roll out the Red Fondant Icing to .5cm thick and 30cm in diameter. Place over the cake moulding in around the sides and cutting a strip off where the head will be.

Roll out the Black Fondant Icing and lay over the head, trim away excess icing.

Cut licorice strap for six legs and strip down the shell. Two licorice twists are pressed into the Black Icing for antennae.

Pipe Buttercream Icing with a No. 2 icing nozzle, for eyes, nose and mouth and a dot on the back of each brown sweet to make it adhere to the Ladybird's wings.

Coconut coloured green could be placed around the Ladybird for colour and realism.

Festivals

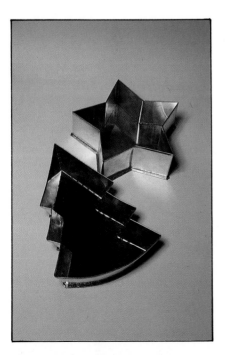

CHRISTMAS TREE

**fruit cake recipe or light sultana
  cake**
1 egg white
300gm marzipan
400gm Green Fondant Icing
Royal Icing
red pebbles
red food colouring
7 candles
santa
tinsel cut into 6 small pieces
ballet dancer
licorice
cachous
Brown Fondant Icing

Bake the cake in this hired Christmas
Tree tin obtained from a Cake
Decorating shop.

To ice the cake beat the egg white
and brush all over the cake. Roll out the
marzipan icing to .5cm thick and lift onto
the tree cake moulding around the
"branches" carefully.

Roll out the Green Fondant Icing in the
same way and place over the marzipan
which has been slightly dampened with
egg white to act as an adhesive.

With White Royal Icing and a star
nozzle pipe the white swirls onto the
cake and stars where the doll, santa,
tinsel, marzipan parcels, pine cones and
pebbles will be placed. Then set these
objects into place. Push the 7 candles
into the end of the branches.

The "parcels" are square pieces of
marzipan which have been piped with
Red Royal Icing and a No. 2 icing
nozzle.

The "pine cones" are brown Fondant
Icing balls clipped with the tips of
scissors to give the scale-like effect.

A large piece of licorice is gently
pushed into the base of the tree to make
a "trunk".

The four candy walking sticks add to
the festive spirit.

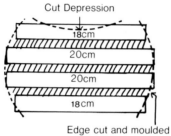

Cut Depression

18cm

20cm

20cm

18cm

Edge cut and moulded
to pumpkin shape

/////////// Cream layers

HALLOWEEN PUMPKIN

1 recipe of chocolate cake
1 recipe of Chocolate Buttercream
   Icing
300ml cream
500gm Orange Fondant Icing
White, Black and Yellow Fondant
   Icings
Black Royal Icing
licorice pipe
candles and toothpicks
1 frog and 2 plastic trees

Bake the chocolate cake recipe in an 18cm round pan and a 20cm round pan.

Cut each cake through the centre and pile the four cakes up with cream and jam as in the diagram. The top and bottom cakes are 18cm diam. and the two inner cakes are 20cm diam. Cut a depression in the top cake for the "stalk" and add this cake to the sides of the pumpkin, trimming and shaping the pumpkin with cake.

Then Buttercream Icing is smoothed all over the cake for extra roundness.

Roll out the Orange Fondant Icing to .5cm thick into a large circle. With a rolling pin carefully lift the fondant onto the cake rounding the curves of the pumpkin and trimming off excess icing. Place a licorice pipe in the top depression.

Make the "ghosts" as in the "No. 5" cake in section 6.

The hollow candles sit on toothpicks which are inserted into the cake not quite horizontally and when they are lit an eerie effect is achieved.

The pumpkin's face is made from cut out pieces of coloured fondant and is adhered to the cake with water. The frog sits on the pumpkin.

Index